The Tulsa Massacre of 1921: The Controversial History and Legacy of America's Worst Race Riot

By Charles River Editors

A picture taken during the riot

About Charles River Editors

Charles River Editors is a boutique digital publishing company, specializing in bringing history back to life with educational and engaging books on a wide range of topics. Keep up to date with our new and free offerings with this 5 second sign up on our weekly mailing list, and visit Our Kindle Author Page to see other recently published Kindle titles.

We make these books for you and always want to know our readers' opinions, so we encourage you to leave reviews and look forward to publishing new and exciting titles each week.

Introduction

A picture taken during the riot on Archer and Greenwood

"Lurid flames roared and belched and licked their forked tongues into the air. Smoke ascended the sky in thick, black volumes and amid it all, the planes – now a dozen or more in number – still hummed and darted here and there with the agility of natural birds of the air." – Eyewitness account

It all began on Memorial Day, May 31, 1921. Around or after 4:00 p.m. that day, a clerk at Renberg's clothing store on the first floor of the Drexel Building in Tulsa heard a woman scream. Turning in the direction of the scream, he saw a young black man running from the building. Going to the elevator, the clerk found the white elevator operator, 17-year-old Sarah Page, crying and distraught. The clerk concluded that she had been assaulted by the black man he saw running a few moments earlier and called the police.

Those facts are just about the only things people agree on when it comes to the riot in Tulsa in 1921. By the time the unrest ended, an unknown number of Tulsa's black citizens were dead, over 800 people were injured, and what had been the wealthiest black community in the United States had been laid to waste.

In the days after the riot, a group formed to work on rebuilding the Greenwood neighborhood, which had been all but destroyed. The former mayor of Tulsa, Judge J. Martin, declared, "Tulsa can only redeem herself from the country-wide shame and humiliation into which she is today plunged by complete restitution and rehabilitation of the destroyed black belt. The rest of the United States must know that the real citizenship of Tulsa weeps at this unspeakable crime and will make good the damage, so far as it can be done, to the last penny."

However, financial assistance would be slow in coming, a jury would find that black mobs were responsible for the damage, and not a single person was ever convicted as a result of the riot. Indeed, given that racist violence directed at blacks was the norm in the Jim Crow South, and accusations of black teens or adults violating young white girls were often accepted without evidence, people barely batted an eye at the damage wrought by the riot, which would remain largely overlooked for almost 70 years. Only in the last two decades have Oklahomans reckoned with this shameful episode in their history.

The Tulsa Massacre of 1921: The Controversial History and Legacy of America's Worst Race Riot examines the conditions and events that led to the riot, the damage done, and the aftermath. Along with pictures depicting important people, places, and events, you will learn about the Tulsa race riot of 1921 like never before.

A Boomtown

The roots of the Tulsa Race Riot lay in the social and economic history of the city of Tulsa itself. Racial intolerance has deep roots in American history, going back to the arrival of the first Africans at Jamestown in 1620. Through slavery and the Civil War, black Americans attained freedom from chattel slavery, but continued to suffer discrimination both legal in the form of Jim Crow laws and de facto in the continued perception among the vast majority of white Americans that African-Americans were at the very least inferior and at the most a constant dangerous presence in their communities who must be carefully controlled. In this way, Tulsa was no different than most cities in the region in the 1920s.

But in one way, Tulsa was different for African-Americans. The city was economically prosperous thanks to a booming oil industry, and despite Jim Crow and racial discrimination, black citizens of the city shared in this wealth, if not as equally as their white neighbors. The Greenwood district, a 36 square block section of northern Tulsa, was considered the wealthiest African-American neighborhood in the country, called the "Black Wall Street" because of the large number of affluent and professional residents. In the 2001 final report of the Oklahoma Commission to Study the Tulsa Race Riot of 1921, historians John Hope Franklin and Scott Ellsworth described the Greenwood area that would be all but destroyed in the riot: "In less than twenty-four hours, nearly all of Tulsa's African-American residential district--some forty-square-blocks in all--had been laid to waste, leaving nearly nine-thousand people homeless. Gone, too, was the city's African-American commercial district, a thriving area located among Greenwood Avenue which boasted some of the finest black-owned businesses in the Southwest. The Stradford Hotel, a modern fifty-four room brick establishment which housed a drug store, barber shop, restaurant and banquet hall, had been burned to the ground. So had the Gurley Hotel, the Red Wing Hotel, and the Midway Hotel. Literally dozens of family-run businesses--from cafes and mom-and-pop grocery stores, to the Dreamland Theater, the Y.M.C.A. cleaners, the East End Feed Store, and Osborne Monroe's roller skating rink--had also gone up in flames, taking with them the livelihoods, and in many cases the life savings, of literally hundreds of people. The offices of two newspapers--the *Tulsa Star* and the *Oklahoma Sun--* had also been destroyed, as were the offices of more than a dozen doctors, dentists, lawyers, realtors, and other professionals. A United States Post Office substation was burned as was the all-black Frissell Memorial Hospital. The brand new Booker T. Washington High School building escaped the torches of the rioters, but Dunbar Elementary School did not. Neither did more than a half dozen African-American churches, including the newly constructed Mount Zion Baptist Church, an impressive brick tabernacle which had been dedicated only seven weeks earlier."

Overall, Tulsa in 1921 was considered a modern, vibrant city overall. The report noted, "Of all the qualities that impressed out-of-town visitors about Tulsa in the days before the race riot, one of them was just how new and up-to-date everything seemed. From the modern office buildings that were rising up out of downtown, to the electric trolleys that rumbled back and forth along

Main Street, to the rows of freshly painted houses that kept pushing the city limits further and further into the surrounding countryside, compared to other cities, Tulsa was nothing short of an overnight sensation. Indeed, Tulsa had grown so much and so fast--in a now-you-don't-see-it, now-you-do kind of fashion--that local boosters called it the Magic City."

What had fueled this remarkable growth was oil, specifically the discovery of the Glenn Pool oil field in 1905. Within five years, Tulsa had grown from a rural crossroads town in the former Indian Territory into a boomtown with more than 10,000 citizens, and as word spread of the fortunes that could be made in Tulsa, people of all races poured into the city. By 1920, the greater Tulsa area boasted a population of over 100,000.

As the hub of the Mid-Continent Oil Field, Tulsa was home to over 400 oil and gas companies, along with oil field supply companies, tank manufacturers, pipeline companies, and refineries. Four different railroads served the city, automobiles sped down modern paved streets, and by 1919, Tulsa boasted a commercial airport. A new county courthouse was built in 1912, a federal building arrived in 1915, and the city hall opened in 1917. To top everything off, the city could boast of a 3,500 seat auditorium completed in 1914. There were two daily newspapers--the *Tulsa World* and *Tulsa Tribune*. Four telegraph companies serviced the city, and Tulsans communicated with each other through some ten-thousand telephones. The town had seven banks as well as dozens of financial firms. There were jewelers, furniture stores, clothiers, motion picture theaters, and scores of other stores for Tulsa's citizens to spend their oil money.

Tulsa's residential neighborhoods were some of the most modern and stylish in the country, and the Tulsa Chamber of Commerce produced postcards and literature boasting of the virtues of life in their modern oil city. However, as the commission report pointed out, "What the pamphlets and the picture postcards did not reveal was that, despite of its impressive new architecture and its increasingly urbane affectations, Tulsa was a deeply troubled town. AS 1920 turned into 1921, the city would soon face a crossroads that, in the end, would change it forever...Tulsa was, in some ways, not one city but two."

African-Americans were among those who flocked to the Tulsa area looking for security and prosperity. Some had lived in the Indian Territory, descendants of the slaves who had accompanied the Creeks, Cherokees, and Choctaws on the Trail of Tears. Others descended from runaway slaves who sought freedom with the Indians before and during the Civil War. Most of Tulsa's black community, however, consisted of newcomers to the state, mostly hailing from Mississippi and Missouri, though some came from as far away as Georgia. The commission report explained, "For many, Oklahoma represented not only a chance to escape the harsher racial realities of life in former states of the Old South, but was literally a land of hope, a place worth sacrificing for, a place to start anew. And come they did, in wagons and on horseback, by train and on foot."

When they came to Tulsa, many blacks settled in the Greenwood area and established a thriving commercial, cultural, and residential area. Of course, the segregation was forced on these residents, and while they had fled the worst conditions of the Jim Crow South in other areas, they were not able to escape it completely. The report noted, "Greenwood was not only the place where black Tulsans chose to shop, but was also practically the only place that they could. Hemmed in by the city's residential segregation ordinance, African-Americans were generally barred from patronizing white-owned stores downtown--or ran the risk of insult, or worse, if they tried. While many black tulsans made a conscious decision to patronize African-American merchants, the fact of the matter was that they had few other places to go."

When Oklahoma was admitted as a state on November 16, 1907, one of the first acts of the state legislature was to pass Jim Crow laws. The very first law passed segregated all rail travel, and voter registration rules disenfranchised most African-Americans. The *Encyclopedia of Oklahoma History* described the variety of laws that were passed: "[T]he first legislature wrote segregation into law with Senate Bill Number One after first defining all people with any degree of African ancestry as black. The solons banned interracial marriages and miscegenation, both of which became felonies. State law also targeted ministers who performed ceremonies for mixed couples; they, too, could be charged with felonies. The legislature banned interracial schools at all levels. Many public facilities along with common carriers were segregated. Some 540 railroad depots in the state had to be altered to fit the new separate waiting rooms requirement, and new coaches also had to be added to the lines. Over time, legislators segregated everything from hospitals to housing to cemeteries to restaurants. In 1915 Oklahoma made national history by becoming the first state in the Union to segregate public pay telephone booths."

Localities passed their own ordinances enforcing segregation, and Tulsa was among them. Inevitably, the location of black housing was one of the issues, and on August 4, 1916, the Tulsa City Council passed an ordinance prohibiting anyone from purchasing a house on a block where 75% or more of the residents were of a different race than the purchasers. Blacks could only live on a majority white block if they were employed as domestic servants at least five days a week on a property on that block. While the U.S. Supreme Court eventually ruled that such zoning ordinances were unconstitutional, cities continued to pass them and Tulsa's remained in force in defiance of the Court. The ordinance justifiably angered the residents of the Greenwood community, adding to growing racial tensions in the city.

In addition to the legal enforcement of white supremacy, white Oklahomans resorted to extrajudicial means of enforcing their power. As in other areas of the country, lynchings of blacks were common whenever criminal accusations flew, regardless of the evidence to back up their validity. The authors of the commission report explained, "In large part owing to conditions of frontier lawlessness, Oklahoma had long been plagued by lynchings, and during the territorial days, numerous suspected horse thieves, cattle rustlers, and outlaws, the vast majority of whom were white, had been lynched by white mobs. However, from 1911 onward, all of the state's lynching victims, save one, were African Americans. And during the next decade, twenty-three black Oklahomans--including two women--were lynched by whites in more than a dozen different Oklahoma communities including Anadarko, Ardmore, Eufaula, Holdenville, Idabel, Lawton, Madill, Mannford, Muldrow, Norman, Nowata, Okemah, Oklahoma city, Purcell, Shawnee, Wagoner, and Wewoka."

The most notorious organized expression of white supremacy at the time came from the Ku Klux Klan. In the early 20th century, the group essentially descended from the original Klan organized by ex-Confederates to resist the Union occupation of the South and suppress the aspirations of freed slaves. The second incarnation of the Klan was organized in 1915 at a meeting on Stone Mountain outside Atlanta, Georgia, in the wake of the Leo Frank case. The new Klan grew slowly during the late 1910s, but after the end of World War I, fears of communist revolution in the United States combined with racial tensions and a fear of "un-American" immigrants spurred an explosion of membership in the organization. Not only was there a growth in numbers, but the Klan spread outside of its traditional home in the former states of the Confederacy into states of the Midwest and Great Plains.

It appears that Klan organizers first arrived in Oklahoma in the summer of 1920, though there is no record of an organized Klan presence in Tulsa until August 1921, two months after the riot. In his dissertation on the history of the Oklahoma Klan, Clark asserted that the Tulsa race riot "greatly assisted...organizational efforts among fearful and angry whites. The Klan could not be credited with precipitating the riot, but some of its members had an intimate relationship with the events." In a speech one month after the riot, a Klansman from Atlanta spoke in Tulsa and said of the riot that it "was the best thing ever happened to Tulsa and that by judging from the way strange Negroes were coming to Tulsa we might have to do it all over again."

Once established, Tulsa became a lively locale for Klan activity. It is estimated that in December 1921, the Tulsa Klan had 3,200 members out of a population of around 72,000 in 1920. Clark described the growth of the Klan in Tulsa: "Kleagles capitalized upon the emotions in the wake of the race riot to propagandize the white community of Tulsa. The result was astounding. Soon the Tulsa Klan Number Two boasted of 2,000 members. The Klavern, the smallest local unit of the organizational structure wherein the ritual ceremonies were held, grew so rapidly that in six months the Klan paid an estimated $60,000 for the Centenary Methodist Church building in Tulsa and built one of the largest meeting halls in the Southwest on the spot. Civil leaders formed formed the Tulsa Benevolent Association in January, 1922. It served as the holding company for the Tulsa Klan under the leadership of the Exalted Cyclops, who was William Shelley Rogers, and included many of the prominent business, professional, and local government leaders of the region. Tulsa gossips passed along the common rumor that all district judges, the court clerk, the county sheriff, and all jury commissioners were members of the Klan."

Given that the growth of the Ku Klux Klan among the white citizens of Tulsa came after the riot, the group itself can't be directly blamed. Instead, the riot was an outgrowth of racial and social tensions in the city that mirrored those in other areas in the aftermath of World War I. The return of black soldiers to urban areas in 1918 prompted worries among whites, who feared that lawless black mobs would threaten the safety and stability of their cities. Riots broke out in Northern cities, with whites rampaging through black commercial and residential areas, burning black-owned properties and killing and injuring men, women and children. One of the worst such riots occurred in Chicago from July 27-August 3, 1919, during which 38 people (23 black, 15 white) died, 537 were injured, and between 1,000 and 2,000 Chicagoans, most of them black, lost their homes.

While there was not an outbreak of racial violence in Tulsa that summer, the pattern of the later riot in that city mirrored that of Chicago, with white mobs rampaging through black areas of the city in response to rumored violence and other activities that (theoretically) defied white supremacy. By 1921, tensions arising from a variety of factors threatened to fan racial animosities. The report commented, "Despite the fact that segregation appeared to be gaining ground statewide, in the months leading up to the riot, more than a few white Tulsans instead feared, at least in Tulsa itself, that the opposite was true. Many were especially incensed when black Tulsans disregarded, or challenged, Jim Crow practices. Others were both enraged at, and jealous of, the material success of some of Greenwood's leading citizens--feelings that were no doubt increased by the sharp drop in the price of crude oil, and the subsequent layoffs in the oil fields, that preceded the riot. Indeed, an unidentified writer for one white Tulsa publication, the Exchange Bureau Bulletin, later listed 'n*****s with money' as one of the so-called causes of the catastrophe. During the weeks and months leading up to the riot, there were more than a few white Tulsans who not only feared that the color line was in danger of being slowly erased, but believed that this was already happening."

Joined with this concern among whites that their dominance was in danger was a growing concern about crime and vice in Tulsa. A federal agent who spent a week undercover in Tulsa in April 1921, a month before the outbreak of the riot, reported, "Gambling, bootlegging and prostitution are very much in evidence. At the leading hotels and rooming houses the bell hops and porters are pimping for women and also selling booze. Regarding violations of the law, these prostitutes and pimps solicit without any fear of the police, as they will invariably remind you that you are safe in these houses...Vice conditions in this city are extremely bad."

Growing concern about crime, particularly violations of prohibition laws, led to an anti-crime movement in the city spurred by the city's newspapers, which editorialized against vice and crime in increasingly racial tones. The *Tulsa Tribune* led the way, but the commission's report claimed, "Despite later claims to the contrary, for much of early 1921, race had not been much of a factor in the *Tribune's* vigorous anti-crime and anti-corruption campaign."

The paper had not highlighted crimes in Greenwood to a greater degree than other areas of the city, nor did they focus on black criminals disproportionately, but the paper stoked racial tensions shortly before the riot occurred that summer: "But beginning on May 21, 1921, only ten days before the riot, all that was to change. In a lengthy, front-page article...not only did racial issues suddenly come to the foreground, but more importantly, they did so in a manner that featured the highly explosive subject of relations between black men and white women...Accompanied by a private detective [Reverend Harold G. Cooke, the white pastor of Centenary Methodist Church] had led a small group of white men on an undercover tour of the city's illicit nightlife--and had been, it was reported, horrified at what he had discovered…Not only was liquor available at every place that they visited, but at hotels and rooming houses across the city. It was said, African American porters rather routinely offered to provide the men with the services of white prostitutes. Just beyond the city limits, the *Tribune* reported, the group visited a roadhouse where the color lines seemed to have disappeared entirely. 'We found whites and Negroes singing and dancing together,' one member of Reverend Cook's party testified, 'Young, white girls were dancing while Negroes played.'"

All of this coverage gave white Tulsans a new target for their concerns: black men who in their view had too much contact with white women. The commission report noted: "By the end of May 1921, an unstable and potentially volatile local atmosphere. For more than a few white Tulsans, local conditions regarding crime and punishment were fast becoming intolerable. Frustrated over the amount of lawbreaking in their city, and by the apparent inability of the police to do anything about it, they had helped turn the city into a ticking time bomb, where anger and frustration sat just beneath the surface, waiting to explode."

At the same time, Greenwood residents had a growing determination themselves: "[T]here were black Tulsans who were more determined than ever than in their city, no African-American would fall victim to mob violence. World War I veterans and newspaper editors, common laborers and businessmen, they were just as prepared as they had been two years earlier to make certain that no black person was ever lynched in Tulsa, Oklahoma."

The pieces were thus in place for an explosion.

The Mob Gathers

Given their importance at the center of events leading to the Tulsa riot, there is very little known about either Dick Rowland or Sara Page.

Rowland, the young black man spotted running from the Drexel Building, is presumed to have been 19 at the time. His place of birth is unknown, but it is known his name at birth was Jimmie Jones, and by 1908 he and his two sisters had been orphaned. Jimmie was taken in by Damie Ford, and around 1909 Ford moved herself and Jimmie to Tulsa and moved in with Ford's family, the Rowlands. Jimmie took Rowland as his last name and adopted Dick as his first name. He attended Booker T. Washington High School, but he dropped out before graduating. Rowland took a job shining shoes at a white-owned and white-patronized shine parlor on Main Street. It was there that he was working on May 30, 1921.

Even less is known about Sarah Page. She was 17-years-old and worked as an elevator operator at the Drexel Building, a job typically reserved for women at the time. It is believed she came to Tulsa from Missouri and lived in a rented room located on North Boston Avenue. There have been reports that she was attending a local business school at the time.

The Drexel Building

The elevator of the Drexel Building that Page operated was the only one in the building, and Rowland would have had a perfectly legitimate reason for wanting to use the elevator. The segregation of facilities in Tulsa was so strict that the shine parlor had no toilet facilities for its black employees. Instead, the owner of the parlor had arranged for his employees to use the closest "Colored" restroom, which happened to be located on the fifth floor of the Drexel

Building. In order to get there, Rowland would have had to use the elevator.

Since the arrangement made by his employer had been in place for a long time, it has led to speculation that Rowland and Page knew each other before that day. The commission report explained, "It seems reasonable that they would have least been able to recognize each other on sight, as Rowland would have regularly ridden in Page's elevator on his way to and from the restroom. Others, however, have speculated that the pair might have been lovers – a dangerous and potentially deadly taboo, but not an impossibility...Whether they knew each other or not, it is clear that both Dick Rowland and Sarah Page were downtown on Monday, May 30, 1921 – although this, too, is cloaked in some mystery. On Memorial Day, most – but not all – stores and businesses in Tulsa were closed. Yet, both Rowland and Page were apparently working that day."

The only thing that is not subject to speculation is that at some point on Memorial Day, Rowland entered the elevator Page was operating in the Drexel Building. It is what happened next that has been the object of speculation since that day. The most commonly believed explanation was that Rowland tripped as he got on the elevator and grabbed Page by the arm to break his fall. Page, likely startled, screamed in response. Those who knew Rowland insisted that this was the most likely explanation, and that the young man would never have been capable of rape.

The clerk working at Renberg's, however, drew the opposite conclusion. Hearing a woman's screams and seeing a young black man appear to run from the building, the clerk rushed to the elevator and found Page. Perceiving her to be distraught, the clerk decided that she was the victim of an attempted sexual assault and called the police.

The official police record is vague about what happened next. The clerk apparently stuck to his story, but there is no record of what Page told the police when they interviewed her. Based on the actions the police took next, it does not appear that whatever Page told them was interpreted as an attempted sexual assault by a black male on a white female. The police did not issue an all-points bulletin for Rowland, but instead kept the investigation low-key. Rowland, for his part, went to his adopted mother's home and hid out, no doubt fearful of being set upon by a white lynch mob.

Whatever investigation the police did, the next morning, May 31, Tulsa police arrested Rowland. One of the arresting officers, Patrolman Henry C. Pack, was among the few black members of the 75 on the city police force. Police booked Rowland at police headquarters, and he was initially held at the city jail. He was moved later that day to the county jail, located on the top floor of the Tulsa County Courthouse, after police received an anonymous threat on Rowland's life. Damie Ford lost no time hiring a prominent white attorney to defend her adopted son. Rowland was known to quite a few of the lawyers in Tulsa who frequented the parlor where he worked, and at least one of the attorneys in town was overheard saying, "I don't believe a damn word of it. Why I know the boy and have known him a good long while. That's not in him."

The courthouse

Eventually, Rowland's arrest caught the attention of the afternoon paper of record in Tulsa, the *Tulsa Tribune*. The *Tribune* published an article about the arrest on its front page with the headline, "Nab Negro for Attacking Girl in an Elevator." Part of the article told readers, "A Negro delivery boy who gave his name to the public as 'Diamond Dick' but who has been identified as Dick Rowland, was arrested on South Greenwood Avenue this morning by Officers Carmichael and Pack, charged with attempting to assault the 17-year-old white elevator girl in the Drexel Building early yesterday. He will be tried in municipal court this afternoon on a state charge. The girl said she noticed the Negro a few minutes before the attempted assault looking up and down the hallway on the third floor of the Drexel Building as if to see if there was anyone in in sight but thought nothing of it at the time. A few minutes later he entered the elevator she claimed, and attacked her, scratching her hands and face and tearing her clothes. Her screams brought a clerk from Renberg's store to her assistance and the Negro fled. He was captured and identified this morning both by the girl and the clerk, police say. Tenants of the Drexel Building said the girl is an orphan who works as an elevator operator to pay her way through business college."

Nab Negro for AttackingGirl In an Elevator

A negro delivery boy who gave his name to the police as "Diamond Dick" but who has been identified as Dick Rowland, was arrested on South Greenwood avenue this morning by Officers Carmichael and Pack, charged with attempting to assault the 17-year-old white elevator girl in the Drexel building early yesterday.

He will be tried in municipal court this afternoon on a state charge.

The girl said she noticed the negro a few minutes before the attempted assault looking up and down the hallway on the third floor of the Drexel building as if to see if there was anyone in sight but thought nothing of it at the time.

A few minutes later he entered the elevator she claimed, and attacked her, scratching her hands and face and tearing her clothes. Her screams brought a clerk from Renberg's store to her assistance and the negro fled. He was captured and identified this morning both by the girl and clerk, police say.

Rowland denied that he tried to harm the girl, but admitted he put his hand on her arm in the elevator when she was alone.

Tenants of the Drexel building said the girl is an orphan who works as an elevator operator to pay her way through business college.

Where the *Tribune* got the description of the incident that they ascribed to Sarah Page is unknown, since there is no known record of such a statement to the police. It is possible this was what they received from the store clerk, or one of the reporters may have simply made it up.

There is a further mystery about what the *Tribune* printed in its pages. There is no complete run of the bound volumes of the newspaper. The microfilm version does contain the issue of

May 31, 1921, but before the issue was microfilmed, the article that appeared on the front page was torn out along with the bulk of the editorial page. A copy was found by Loren Gill for his 1946 Master's thesis on the riot and reprinted in its entirety, and another copy is in the Red Cross papers that are part of the collections of the Tulsa Historical Society. A copy of what was printed on the editorial page has never been located, however.

Witnesses to the events surrounding the riot remembered the *Tribune* mentioning the possibility of a lynching. One person recalled, in an interview shortly after the riot, "The *Daily Tribune*, a white newspaper that tries to gain its popularity by referring to the Negro settlement as 'Little Africa,' came out on the evening of Tuesday, May 31, with an article claiming that a Negro had experienced some trouble with a white elevator girl at the Drexel Building, it also said that a mob of whites was forming in order to lynch the Negro."

The talk of lynching Rowland was reported shortly after the *Tribune* report. By 4:00, Police and Fire Commissioner J.F. Adkinson telephoned Sheriff Willard McCullough and alerted him to the rumors. Fueling these rumors, a crowd of white residents began to gather around the Tulsa County Courthouse at Sixth and Boulder, and by sunset the crowd had swelled to several hundred. The new sheriff of Tulsa County, Willard M. McCullough, took steps to ensure Rowland's safety. He organized his deputies in a defensive perimeter around the prisoner, disabled the building's elevator, positioned six deputies with rifles and shotguns on the roof, and ordered his remaining men to guard the top of the stairs and shoot anyone on sight. McCullough stood on the courthouse steps and tried to get the mob to go home, but he was reportedly shouted down. Three men entered the courthouse and demanded the sheriff turn Rowland over before they were turned away.

McCullough

The Riot

While the white mob was surrounding the courthouse and Sheriff McCullough was doing his best to protect Rowland's life, news of what was going on spread to Greenwood. There was some dispute among the community as to the proper response to take. At the Dreamland Theater, a man jumped onto the stage. "We're not going to let this happen," he declared. "We're going to go downtown and stop this lynching. Close this place down." B. C. Franklin later recalled two war veterans exhorting a crowd to go downtown to stop the lynching. The commission report explained, "What went unspoken was the fact an African-American had never been lynched in Tulsa. How to prevent one from taking place now was no easy matter...exactly how to respond was of utmost concern." A.J. Smitherman, editor of the *Tulsa Star*, urged action, saying, "Come on boys, let's go downtown."

On the other hand, O. W. Gurley, the owner of the Gurley Hotel, and Barney Cleaver, a black deputy sheriff, counseled caution. Gurley would later tell the grand jury investigating the riot, "I saw a bunch of negroes the night of the riot starting up town and I told them to go back home; the first knowledge I had of it was from Mr. A. F. Bryant; I went upstairs and when I came back down I saw John Smithisen, and he said we will go to the Star office; I went away and when I came back in ¾ of an hour 50 or 60 men were armed with rifles; I asked them to go home, and told them there was no danger of a lynching, and one fellow said that is a damn lie, Mr. McCullough just called for us."

What happened next is somewhat murky. Grand jury testimony would later claim that a group of 50 or 60 black veterans armed with rifles and shotguns arrived at the jail to support Sheriff McCullough (the commission report decades later put the number at 25). In any event, regardless of the exact number, the men marched from their cars to the courthouse steps. Attorney General James Luther would later tell the grand jury, "I saw a car full of negroes driving through the streets with guns; I saw Bill McCullough and told him those negroes would cause trouble; McCullough tried to talk to them, and they got out and stood in single file. W. G. Daggs was killed near Boulder and Sixth street. I was under the impression that a man with authority could have stopped and disarmed them. I saw Chief of Police on south side of court house on top step, talking; I did not see any officer except the Chief; I walked in the court house and met McCullough in about 15 feet of his door; I told him these negroes were going to make trouble, and he said he had told them to go home; he went out and told the whites to go home, and one said 'they said you told them to come up here.' McCullough said 'I did not' and a negro said you did tell us to come."

McCullough was able to persuade the men that Rowland was safe, and that there was no danger of him being turned over to be lynched. Satisfied, the men returned to Greenwood, but the sight of armed black men incited the white mob, which now numbered an estimated 1,000 people. Many of the whites went home to retrieve their own guns, and some headed to the National Guard Armory.

Major James A. Bell, who had already alerted his guardsmen to report to the armory in case they were needed, was informed that a mob of white men was attempting to break into the armory. He later reported, "About 9 o'clock P M. on May 31st. Two members of the guard...came to my door and reported that a crowd of white mem were gathering near the Court House, and that threats of lynching a negro were being made, and that it was reported the negroes in 'Little Africa' were arming to prevent it. As I had heard rumors of this kind on other occasions that did not amount to anything serious I did not feel greatly worried. However, I instructed these men to return to town and get all the information they could; see what the crowd was doing; whether they were armed or not and report back to me at the Armory. I then went to the Armory and called up the Sheriff and asked if there was any indications of trouble down there. The sheriff reported that there were some threats but did not believe it would amount to anything, that in any event he could protect his prisoner. I then called the Chief of Police and asked him the same questions. The chief reported that things were a little threatening, that it was reported that negroes were driving around town in a threatening mood. I then notified the commanding officers of the three Tulsa units, who were in the Armory getting ready for camp, to hold all men in the Armory, have them get into their uniforms, get all arms and ammunition ready so that if it became necessary and the Governor called us we would be ready. I, also, notified them to quickly, but quietly, notify all members of the guard to report at the Armory without giving an alarm. I then returned to my home, just across the alley from the Armory, for my uniform. However, before I could get into it a runner came to my door very much excited and reported that a mob was trying to break into the Armory. Grabbing my pistol in one hand and my belt in the other I jumped out of the back door and running down the west side of the Armory building I saw several men apparently pulling at the window grating. Commanding these men to get off the lot and seeing this command obeyed I went to the front of the building near the southwest corner where I saw a mob of white men about three or four hundred strong. I asked them what they wanted. One of them replied 'Rifles and ammunition'. I explained to them that they could not get anything there. Some one shouted 'we don't know about that, we guess we can'. I told them we only had sufficient arms and ammunition for our men and that not one piece could go out of there without orders from the Governor, and in the name of the law demanded that they disperse at once. They continued to press forward in a threatening manner when with drawn pistol I again demanded that they disperse and explained that the men in the Armory were armed with rifles loaded with ball ammunition and that they would shoot promptly to prevent any unauthorized person entering there. By maintaining a firm stand...the mob was dispersed."

Back at the courthouse, the crowd had swelled to more than 2,000 people by 9:30 pm. Reverend Charles W. Kerr of the First Presbyterian Church, among other local leaders, tried to get the mob to disperse. The Police Chief, John A. Gustafson, later claimed that he tried to talk the lynch mob into dispersing, but he was not on the scene by 10:00.

As the evening wore on, blacks in Greenwood became increasingly concerned. Small groups would venture by car to the courthouse to keep tabs on what was going on, and many of the whites at the courthouse interpreted these actions as the beginning of a "negro uprising." At 10:00 p.m., a larger group of armed men, perhaps 75 or more, drove from Greenwood to the courthouse to once again offer their services.

It was at this point that the situation escalated. The commission report described the scene: "As the black men were leaving the courthouse for the second time, a white man approached a tall African-American World War I veteran who was carrying an army-issued revolver. 'N*****,' the white man said, 'What are you doing with that pistol?' 'I'm going to use it if I need to,' replied the black veteran. 'No, you give it to me.' 'Like hell I will.' The white man tried to take the gun away from the veteran, and a shot rang out. America's worst race riot had begun. While the first shot fired at the courthouse may have been unintentional, those that followed were not. Almost immediately, members of the white mob--and possibly some law enforcement officers--opened fire on the African-American men, who returned volleys of their own. The initial gunplay lasted only a few seconds, but when it was over, an unknown number of people--perhaps as many as a dozen--both black and white, lay dead or wounded."

The black men retreated toward Greenwood with the white mob in close pursuit, while another skirmish broke out at Second and Cincinnati. Although they were outnumbered and suffering some casualties during the retreat, the black men were able to make it to safety in Greenwood.

The white mob around the courthouse now transformed itself from a lynch mob focused on one black prisoner to one looking to take out their frustrations on any black target they could. They began to move along the sidewalks downtown, and one witness would later say, “A great many of these persons lining the sidewalks were holding a rifle or shotgun in one hand, and grasping the neck of a liquor bottle with the other. Some had pistols stuck into their belts.” Many were sworn in by police officers as “Special Deputies.” Groups of whites began breaking into downtown sporting goods stores and pawnshops to get guns and ammunition.

Armed whites then began gunning down any black person they found downtown. William R. Holway, a white engineer, was watching a movie at the Rialto Theater when someone ran into the theater yelling, “N***** fight! N***** fight!” He recalled, “Everybody left that theater on high, you know. We went out the door and looked across the street, and there was Younkman’s drug store with those big pillars. There were two big pillars. There were two big pillars at the entrance, and we got over behind them. Just got there when a Negro ran south of the alley across the street, the minute his head showed outside, somebody shot him. We stood there for about half-an-hour watching which I shall never forget. He wasn’t quite dead, but he was about to die. He was the first man I saw shot in that riot.”

A white teenager, William Phillips, later described a similar event in the Royal Theater: “The mob action was set off when several [white] men chased a Negro man down the alley in back of the theater and out onto Fourth Street where he saw the stage door and dashed inside. Seeing the open door the Negro rushed in and hurried forward in the darkness hunting a place to hide. Suddenly he was on the stage in front of the picture screen and blinded by the bright flickering light coming down from the operator’s booth in the balcony. After shielding his eyes for a moment he regained his vision enough to locate the steps leading from the stage down past the orchestra pit to the aisle just as the pursuing men rushed the stage. One of them saw the Negro and yelled, ‘There he is, heading for the aisle.’ As he finished the sentence, a roaring blast from a shotgun dropped the Negro man by the end of the orchestra pity.”

Sporadic fighting took place throughout the night of May 31-June 1. From midnight until 1:30 a.m., blacks and whites exchanged gunfire across the Frisco yards. A few carloads of whites made excursions into Greenwood, firing into businesses and residences. Walter White, visiting Tulsa immediately after the riot, reported, “Many are the stories of horror told to me--not by colored people--but by white residents. One was that of an aged colored couple, saying their evening prayers before retiring in their little home on Greenwood Avenue. A mob broke into the house, shot both of the old people in the backs of their heads, blowing their brains out and spattering them over the bed, pillaged the home, and then set fire to it.”

Whites began burning black homes and businesses along Archer Street, and then they forced away firefighters who arrived to battle the flames. One firefighter later recounted, "It would mean a fireman's life to turn a stream of water on one of those negro buildings. They shot at us all morning when we were trying to do something but none of my men were hit. There is not a chance in the world to get through that mob into the negro district." Two dozen black-owned businesses burned by 4:00 a.m.

Word began to filter back to Greenwood and other black neighborhoods that angry whites were preparing to invade the district. One such report got back to Seymour Williams, a teacher at Booker T. Washington High School and veteran, compelling him to grab his service revolver and alert his neighbors. In another part of Greenwood, theater owner John Wesley Williams loaded his 30-30 rifle and repeating shotgun, positioning himself in the window of his family's second floor apartment at the corner of Greenwood and Archer. Other black Tulsans decided to leave, and in the early hours of June 1 a steady stream left the city. There was widespread confusion as to what was going on throughout the city, but the uncertainty added to the tensions.

In white neighborhoods, groups of armed men began making plans for what to do next. Phillips would later write, "Many people were drifting out of the restaurant so we decided to go along and see what happened at the meeting place. Driving south on boulder we realized that many trucks and automobiles were headed for the same location, and near Fifteenth Street people had abandoned their vehicles because the streets and intersections were filled to capacity. We left the car more than a block away and began walking toward the crowded intersection. There were already three or four hundred people there and more arriving when we walked up."

After he and his friends arrived there, Phillips noted that a man stood up on top of a car and told the crowd, "We have decided to go out to Second and Lewis Streets and join the crowd that is meeting there." Phillips and his friends returned to their cars and headed east with a long line of cars toward Second and Lewis. There, men were shouting instructions to the crowds. One said, "Men, we are going in at daylight." Another told the crowd, "If any of you have more ammunition than you need, or if what you have doesn't fit your gun, sing out." "Be ready at daybreak," a man urged the crowd, adding, "Nothing can stop us for there will be thousands of others going in at the same time."

Meanwhile, state officials in Oklahoma City were learning of the situation in Tulsa. The commission report explained, "At 10:14 pm, Adjutant General Charles F. Barrett, the commandant of the Oklahoma National Guard, had received a long distance telephone call from Major Byron Kirkpatrick, a Tulsa guard officer, advising him of the worsening conditions in Tulsa. Kirkpatrick phoned again at 12:35 a.m. At that point he was instructed by Governor J.B.A. Robertson to prepare and send a signed telegram, as required by Oklahoma state law, by the chief of police, the county sheriff, and a local judge, requesting that state troops be sent to Tulsa. Kirkpatrick, however, ran into some problems as he tried to collect the necessary signatures, particularly that of Sheriff McCullough, who was still barricaded with his men and Dick Rowland on the top floor of the courthouse. However, Kirkpatrick persevered, and at 1:46 a.m. the needed telegram arrived at the state capital."

At 2:15, Adjutant General Barrett told Kirkpatrick that the governor had authorized calling out the National Guard, and a train of nearly 100 guardsmen would be leaving Oklahoma City for Tulsa at 5:00 that morning.

By sunrise on June 1, groups of armed whites numbering in the thousands had gathered in three clusters on the northern fringes of the downtown area opposite Greenwood. Some observers at would later estimate the total number between 5,000-10,000. One small group of men placed a machine gun at the top of Middle State's Milling Company's grain elevator, positioning it to fire on Greenwood Avenue.

In Greenwood, blacks were faced with a stark choice: fight or flee. What happened to Julia Duff, a teacher at Booker T. Washington High School, was later described in a letter in the *Chicago Defender*: "Mrs. S. came into her room and told her to dress-there was something wrong for soldiers were all around, and she looked out the window and saw them driving the men out of the houses on Detroit. Saw Mr. Wood running with both hands in the air and their 3-month-old baby in one hand and three brutes behind him with guns. She said her legs gave way from under her and she had to crawl about the room, taking things from her closet, putting them in her trunk, for she thought if anything happened she'd have her trunk packed, and before she got everything in they heard footsteps on their steps and there were six out there and they ordered Mr. Smart to march, hands up, out of the house."

Eyewitnesses recalled that around dawn that morning at 5:08 am, there was a whistle or siren that could be heard. Moments later, the white mobs began to move, the machine gun on the elevator opened fire, and crowds of whites headed straight for the commercial district. One witness recalled, "With wild frenzied shouts, men began pouring from behind the freight depot and the long string of boxcars and evidently from behind the piles of oil well easing which was at the other end and on the north side of the building. From every place of shelter up and down the tracks came screaming, shouting men to join in the rush toward the Negro section. Mingled with the shouting were a few rebel-yells and Indian gobblings as the great wave of humanity rushed forward totally absorbed in thoughts of destruction." As reporter Mary Parish later put it, "Tuesday Night, May 31, was the riot, and Wednesday morning, by daybreak, was the invasion."

Faced with the overwhelming numbers of whites, the black residents of Greenwood who had initially resolved to defend their homes and businesses now rushed to leave the district, escaping just ahead of the rampaging mob. The experience of Mary Parrish and her young daughter Florence was typical: "My friend, Mrs. Jones, called her husband, who was trying to take a little rest. They decided to try to make for a place of safety, so called to me that they were leaving. By this time the enemy was close upon us, so they ran out of the south door, which led out onto Archer Street, and went east toward Lansing. I took my little girl, Florence Mary, by the hand and fled out of the west door on Greenwood. I did not take time to get a hat for myself or Baby, but started out north on Greenwood, running amidst showers of bullets from the machine gun located in the granary and from men who were quickly surrounding our district. Seeing that they were fighting at a disadvantage, our men had taken shelter in the buildings and in other placed out of sight of the enemy. When my daughter, Florence Mary, and I ran into the street, it was vacant for a block or more. Someone called to me to 'Get out of the street with that child or you both will be killed.' I felt that it was suicide to remain in the building, for it would surely be destroyed and death in the street was preferred, for we expected to be shot down at any moment. So we placed our trust in God, our Heavenly Father, who seeth and knoweth all things, and ran out of Greenwood in the hope of reaching a friend's home who lived over the Standpipe Hill in Greenwood Addition."

As the sun rose, airplanes began to appear overhead. Eyewitnesses reported that the planes, manned by armed whites, flew low to the ground and shot at fleeing blacks. The commission reported noted that the eyewitness accounts are fairly consistent: "Numerous other eyewitnesses--both black and white--confirm the presence of an unknown number of airplanes flying over Greenwood during the early daylight hours of June 1. While certain other assertions made over the years such as that the planes dropped streams of liquid fire on top of African-American homes and businesses appear to have been technologically improbably, particularly during the early 1920s, there is little doubt but that some of the occupants of the airplanes fired upon black Tulsans with pistols and rifles. Moreover, there is evidence to suggest that men in at least one airplane dropped some dynamite, upon a group of African-American refugees as they were fleeing the city."

As the invasion of the Greenwood district unfolded, a pattern began to emerge that the report later described: "First, the armed whites broke into the black homes and businesses, forcing the occupants out into the street, where they were led away at gunpoint to one of a growing number of internment centers. Anyone who resisted was shot. Moreover, African-American men in homes where firearms were discovered met the same fate. Next, the whites looted the homes and businesses, pocketing small items, and hauling away larger items either on foot or by car or truck. Finally, the white rioters then set the homes and other buildings on fire, using torches and oil-soaked rags. House by house, block by block, the wall of flame crept northward, engulfing the city's black neighborhoods."

Witnesses reported that uniformed police and National Guard, rather than seeking to protect life and property, actively engaged in the rioting. These men, along with armed white civilians, also engaged in activities that led to the imprisonment of virtually all of Tulsa's black citizens. James West, a teacher at Booker T. Washington High School, described his arrest by whites at his home on Easton Street: "Some men appeared with drawn guns and ordered all of the men out of the house. I went out immediately. They ordered me to raise my hands, after which three or four men searched me. They told me to line up in the street. I requested them to let me get my hat and best shoes, but they refused and abusively ordered me to line up. They refused to let one of the men put on any kind of shoes. After lining up some 30 or 40 of us men, they ran us through the streets to Convention Hall, forcing us to keep our hands in the air all the while.

While we were running, some of the ruffians would shoot at our heels and swore at those who had difficulty keeping up. They actually drove a car into the bunch and knocked down two or three men."

A picture of the National Guard with some wounded men during the riot

A picture of "Little Africa" on fire

A panorama of damage taken from Booker T. Washington High School

A picture of damage done on one of Greenwood's residential blocks

The experience of the respected black surgeon Dr. A. C. Jackson is an example of the atrocities Tulsa's whites meted out on their black neighbors. Jackson was shot by whites and eventually succumbed to his injuries. White attorney John A. Oliphant later testified,

Q. About what time in the morning did you say it was Dr. Jackson was shot?

A. Right close to eight o'clock, between seven thirty and eight o'clock.

Q, Dr. Jackson was a Negro?

A. Yes, sir.

Q. And he was coming toward you and these other men at the time he was shot?

A. Yes, sir, coming right between his house, right in his yard between his home and the house below him.

Q. What did these men say at the time he was shot?

A. They didn't say anything but they pulled down on him; I kept begging him not to shoot him, I held him a good bit and I thought he wouldn't shoot but he shot him twice and the other fellow on the other side-and he fell-shot him and broke his leg.

Q. One man shot him twice?

A. Yes, sir, this is my recollection now.

Q. Then another one shot him through the leg?

A. Yes, I didn't look at that fellow.

Q. These same men that shot him carried him to the hospital?

A. No, they didn't.

Q. What did they do?

A. I have never seen them after that, I don't know a thing about what became of them.

Not all of Tulsa's whites participated in the massacre in the Greenwood area. There are many reports of whites acting heroically to save blacks fleeing the violence. The home of Merrill and Ruth Phelps became a refuge for blacks fleeing Tulsa, as the couple hid and fed refugees in the basement of their home for days. Some whites in Tulsa put their own lives at risk to hide blacks from the rioters, including confronting the armed mobs. Mary Jo Erhard, a white stenographer who lived at the Y.W. C. A., hid the organization's black porter in the building's walk-in refrigerator. She later recalled, "Hardly had I hidden him behind the beef carcasses and returned to the hall door when a loud pounding at the service entrance drew me there. A large man was trying to open the door, fortunately securely locked, and there on the stoop stood three very rough-looking middle aged white men, each pointing a revolver in my general direction! 'What do you want?' I asked sharply. Strangely, those guns frightened me not at all. I was so angry I could have torn those ruffians apart-three armed white men chasing one lone, helpless Negro. I cannot recall in all my life feeling hatred toward any person, until then. Apparently my feelings did not show, for one answered, 'Where did he go?' 'Where did WHO go?' I responded. 'That nigger,' one demanded, 'did you let him in here?' 'Mister,' I said, 'I'm not letting ANYBODY in here!,' which was perfectly true. I had already let in all I intended. It was at least ten minutes before I felt secure enough to release Jack...H was nearly frozen, dressed thinly as he was for the hot summer night, but he was ALIVE!"

The smoke rising from the burning Greenwood area could be seen for miles, and it was already thick in the air when the State National Guard finally arrived in Tulsa from Oklahoma City, the train pulling into Tulsa's Frisco and Santa Fe depot at around 9:15. Their arrival did not put an immediate end to the riot, however, because for reasons that are still unclear, the State Troops did not proceed to the Greenwood area. The commission report found, "The reasons for this seeming hold-up appear to be largely due to the fact that certain steps needed to be fulfilled--either through protocol or by law--in order for martial law to be declared in Tulsa. Accordingly, after detraining at the Frisco and Santa Fe station, Adjutant General Barrett led a detachment of soldiers to the courthouse, where an unsuccessful attempt was made to contact Sheriff McCullough. Barrett then went to city hall, where, after conferring with city officials, he contacted Governor Robertson in Oklahoma City and asked to be granted the authority to proclaim martial law in Tulsa County. Other detachments of State Troops, meanwhile, appear to have begun taking charge of black Tulsans who were being held by armed white civilians. However, another account of the riot, published a decade later, alleges that upon their arrival in Tulsa, the State Troops wasted valuable minutes by taking time to prepare and eat breakfast."

Martial law was finally declared in Tulsa at 11:29 a.m., but by this time, the riot had mostly run its course. There were scattered bands of white rioters continuing to loot and burn, but most of the mob had already gone home, while most of the city's black population continued to be held under armed guard at the Convention Hall, the baseball park, and the fairgrounds. As men, women, and children who had fled to the countryside began to come back into town, they were taken into custody.

Following the declaration of martial law, the State Troop finally began to move into what remained of Tulsa's black neighborhoods. There, they disarmed whites and sent them home. Additional detachments of State Troops arrived from other cities throughout June 1, and the streets were eventually cleared. Businesses were ordered to close by 6:00 p.m., and all people except military or civil authorities, physicians, or relief workers were ordered off the streets by 7:00 p.m. By 8:00 p.m. on June 1, order had been restored to the city of Tulsa.

After the riots, the actions of the State Troops were largely praised by black Tulsans. Mary Parrish wrote, "Everyone with whom I met was loud in praise of the State Troops who so gallantly came to the rescue of stricken Tulsa. They used no partiality in quieting the disorder. It is the general belief that if they had reached the scene sooner, many lives and valuable property would have been saved."

The Legacy of the Riot

Soon after the end of the riot came the process of burying the dead. Walter White noted, "O.T. Johnson, commandant of the Tulsa Citadel of the Salvation Army, stated that on Wednesday and Thursday the Salvation Army got thirty-seven Negroes employed as grave diggers and twenty on Friday and Saturday. During the first two days these men dug 120 graves in each of which a dead Negro was buried. No coffins were used. The bodies were dumped into the holes and covered over with dirt."

The commission report found that funeral home records would confirm that black victims were buried in unmarked graves at Oaklawn Cemetery. Oral sources cited additional unmarked graves at Newblock Park, Sand Springs road, and Booker T. Washington Cemetery. According to the report, "Largely buried by strangers, there would be no headstones or graveside services for most of black Tulsa's riot dead. Nor would family members be present at the burials, as most of them were still being held under armed guard at the various detention centers. It appears that in some cases, not only did some black Tulsa families not learn how their loved ones died, but not even where they were buried."

As the dead were buried, the living returned to what remained of Greenwood, and the report discussed what they found: "What they found was a blackened landscape of vacant lots and empty streets, charred timbers and melted metal, ashes and broken dreams. Where the African-American commercial district once stood was now a ghost town of crumbling brick storefronts and the burned-out bulks of automobiles. Gone was the Dreamland and the Dixie, gone was the *Tulsa Star* and the black public library, gone was the Liberty Cafe and Elliott & Hooker's clothing store, H.L. Byars' cleaners and Mabel Little's beauty salon. Gone were literal lifetimes of sweat and hard work, and hard-won rungs on the ladder of the American Dream. Gone, too, were hundreds of homes, and more than a half-dozen African-American churches, all torched by the white invaders. Nearly ten-thousand Tulsans, practically the entire black community, was now homeless."

A postcard of a resident standing outside his destroyed home

News of what occurred in Tulsa spread across the country and was reported in major American newspapers. The reaction in the *New York Times* was typical of many: "The Tulsa race riot has been described as the worst outbreak of the kind in the history of the country. In some of its features it is certainly the most amazing. The attack of a young negro upon a white woman and the gathering of a small force of armed negroes do not account for the running fight for hours and the deliberate burning of the negro quarter, a square mile of buildings, including a church. The cause must lie deeper. Friction between the whites and negroes has been growing in Oklahoma. It is not altogether racial; in part it is economic. During the war Southern negroes flocked to the border State and found profitable employment. There has not been so much for them to do of late, and many of them are loafing on the streets. Not only the idle, shiftless and disorderly have worn out their welcome. It has become a common saying that 'Oklahoma is a white man's country.' When they had plenty of money to spend the negroes bought automobiles, lived high and claimed social privileges that the whites were not inclined to allow them. Drafted for service in France and praised for their patriotism, they naturally had a better opinion of themselves. All these things contributed to fan the flame of racial antagonism. The savage outburst at Tulsa leaves no room for doubt that the rough element among the whites was ripe for a rising to teach the negroes their place. Among the negroes were leaders who were ready for resistance. Unfortunately, when the explosion came the police force was found wanting and the Mayor was slow to call upon the Governor for troops. If the Tulsa collision, with its casualties and destruction of property, had occurred at Vera Cruz, the American people would have deplored the lawlessness of the Mexicans and found it shocking. It will be a bad sign if they are not made uneasy by the Oklahoma exhibition of violence and ferocity. There must be an end of that sort of thing if an approach to anarchy is to be escaped."

Governor James B.A. Robertson called for a grand jury to investigate the events surrounding the events in Tulsa. The grand jury investigation began on June 9 and continued for 12 days, with State Attorney General S. P. Freeling calling numerous witnesses. 85 individuals were indicted, and an all-white jury issued a final report.

Much to the chagrin of black Tulsans, and in the face of all evidence, the report blamed black mobs for the riot. It said in part, "We find that the recent race riot was the direct result of an effort on the part of a certain group of colored men who appeared at the courthouse on the night of May 31, 1921, for the purpose of protecting one Dick Rowland then and now in the custody of the Sheriff of Tulsa county for an alleged assault upon a young white woman. We have not been able to find any evidence either from white or colored citizens that any organized attempt was made or planned to take from the Sheriff's custody any prisoner; the crowd assembled about the courthouse being purely spectators and curiosity seekers resulting from rumors circulated about the city...There was no mob spirit among the whites, no talk of lynching and no arms. The assembly was quietly until the arrival of armed negroes, which precipitated and was the direct cause of the entire affair."

Robertson

The commission report seized on the miscarriage of justice, pointing out that "while a handful of African-Americans were charged with riot-related offences no white Tulsan was ever sent to prison for the murders and burnings of May 31, and June 1, 1921. In the 1920s Oklahoma courtrooms and halls of government, there would be no day of reckoning for either perpetrators or the victims of the Tulsa race riot."

In the wake of the riot, Dick Rowland, whose arrest had set the horrific chain of events into motion, had the charges against him dropped in September after the County Attorney received a letter from Sarah Page stating she did not wish to prosecute the case. According to Damie Ford, Rowland left for Kansas City, and after that, virtually nothing else is known about the rest of Rowland's life.

In much the same way, the decades following the riot saw the memory of it recede into the background. In effect, the Black Wall Street Massacre was shoved down the "memory hole," a device used in George Orwell's *1984* to censor things Big Brother decided needed to be censored. The *Tulsa Tribune* did not recognize the riot in its "Fifteen Years Ago Today" or "Twenty-five Years Ago Today" features. In 1971, the Tulsa Chamber of Commerce decided to commemorate the riot, but when they read the materials gathered by Ed Wheeler about the riot, they refused to publish any of it, and the Tulsa papers also refused to run Wheeler's story. He finally published an article in a black magazine, *Impact Magazine*; but most of Tulsa's white citizens never knew about it.

Mozella Franklin Jones, the daughter of black attorney Buck Colbert Franklin, himself a survivor of the riot, worked tirelessly to raise awareness of the riot in Tulsa and at large. Her efforts helped integrate the Tulsa Historical Society, which mounted the first ever major exhibition on the history of Tulsa's black community and created the first collection of riot photographs available to the public.

Publications about the riot slowly revived public awareness in the event. The first scholarly examination of the event was a Master's thesis written by Loren L. Gill in 1946 at the University of Tulsa. Kay M. Teall's 1971 book, *Black History in Oklahoma*, paid significant attention to the riot, as did Arthur Tolson's 1972 work, *The Black Oklahomans.* In 1975, Rudia M. Halliburton, Jr. published *The Tulsa Race War of 1921*, the first major published study of the massacre.

As the 75th anniversary of the riot neared in 1996, the Oklahoma State Legislature authorized a commission to investigate that dark chapter in state history. The commission conducted interviews and heard testimony from witnesses, and it also undertook archeological, non-invasive ground surveys of Newblock Park, Oaklawn Cemetery, and Booker T. Washington Cemetery. When the commission issued its final report, the transmittal letter said, "This Commission fully understands that it is neither judge nor jury. We have no binding legal authority to assign culpability, to determine damages, to establish a remedy, or to order either restitution or reparations. However, in our interim report in February 2000 the majority of Commissioners declared that reparations to the historic Greenwood community in real and tangible form would be good public policy and do much to repair the emotional and physical scars of this terrible incident in our shared past. We listed several recommended courses of action including direct payments to riot survivors and descendants; a scholarship fund available to students affected by the riot; establishment of an economic development enterprise zone in the historic Greenwood district; a memorial for the riot victims."

In her epilogue to the commission's final report, State Senator Maxine Horner wrote, "On June 1, 1921, Lady Justice was blind. Indeed, her eyes were gouged out. As significant, accumulation of wealth was halted and the community was again left to begin again only with its own meager resources. What is owed this community 80 years later is a repairing--education and economic incentives and something more than symbolic gestures or an official report as an apology extended to the survivors. The climate was real and official. The words of Mayor T. D. Evans spoken during the June 14, 1921 meeting of the Tulsa City Commission are brought to our attention once again: '[T]his uprising was inevitable. If that be true and this judgment had come upon us, then I say it was good generalship to let the destruction come to that section where the trouble was hatched up, put in motion and where it had its inception. All regret the wrongs that fell upon the innocent Negroes and they should receive such help as we can give them. It...is true of any warfare that the fortunes of war fall upon the innocent along with the guilty. This is true on any conflict, invasion, or uprising...Let us immediately get to the outside the fact that everything is quiet in our city, that this menace has been fully conquered, and that we are going on in a normal condition.' The mayor had his way. The conspiracy of silence was launched. We can be proud of our state for reexamining this blot on our state and our conscience, and for daring to place the light from this report on those dark days. This has been an epic journey. It can be an epic beginning. There are chapters left to write. To face, not hide again, the shame from this evil...The Oklahoma legislature is now the caretaker of this past and may disperse to the future forgiving, fair, kind, deserved and decent justice."

Horner

On June 1, 2001, Governor Frank Keating signed the 1921 Tulsa Race Riot Reconciliation Act into law. The bill failed to enact the commission's recommendations for reparations, but in addition to acknowledging that the event occurred and accepting the responsibility of state and local authorities in failing to prevent the violence and loss of life, the bill provided for 300 college scholarships for the descendants of Greenwood residents, economic development in Greenwood, and the creation of a memorial to those who died in the riot. In March 2001, Tulsa Mayor Kathy Taylor held a ceremony where she awarded 118 known survivors gold-plated medals with the state seal. In October 2010, the John Hope Franklin Reconciliation Park was dedicated to the memory of the victims of the riot.

Keating

Taylor

Marc Carlson's picture of John Hope Franklin Reconciliation Park

As the 100th anniversary of the massacre approaches in 2021, the city of Tulsa is still working to complete the historical record. The 2001 commission had arranged for archeological surveys of Newblock Park, Oaklawn Cemetery, and Booker T. Washington Cemetery, which witnesses had identified as possible locations for mass graves of black victims. Investigations of the sites were performed in 1997 and 1998, and preliminary data suggested there were no mass graves in these locations. Further investigations were carried out beginning in October 2019, and on December 17, 2019, the team of forensic archaeologists made an announcement that was reported in the *Washington Post*: "A team of forensic archaeologists who spent weeks using ground-penetrating radar at three sites in the city announced Monday night they found 'anomalies' consistent with mass graves that warrant further testing. The scientists said they detected the anomalies beneath the ground at Oaklawn Cemetery and an area in Tulsa called the 'The Canes,' where the Interstate 244 bridge crosses the Arkansas River. They recommended further radar survey and physical excavation of the sites. Phoebe Stubblefield, a forensic anthropologist from the University of Florida who specializes in human remains identification, called the findings promising, but also cautioned that 'we don't know what lies beneath.' Scott Hammerstedt, a scientist who worked on the geophysical survey, said at Oaklawn 'there are quite a lot of anomalies here consistent with mass graves' near a part of the cemetery where city records show 18 black people were buried in June 1921. In another section of the cemetery, they discovered 'what very much looks like a human-dug pit,' Hammerstedt said. 'This is very likely candidate to be a mass burial. We may need to investigate further.' Tulsa officials had said earlier that the next phase of the investigation could include excavation and an investigation by the State of Oklahoma's Medical Examiner's Office into causes of death. 'The cause of death determination would be an important step to the investigation,' city officials said in a statement, 'as remains will be close to 100 years old and a Spanish Influenza outbreak occurred in Tulsa in 1919 prior to the Race Massacre in 1921.' If mass graves were found, the city and oversight committee — which is made up of descendants of massacre victims, community leaders, historians and scholars — would decide on next steps, city officials said, 'as it relates to storing remains, DNA testing and genealogical research, and commemorating the grave sites and honoring the remains.' Tulsa City Councilor Vanessa Hall-Harper sat in the Carver Middle School auditorium with about 300 other people as the investigators presented their findings. She said she felt a sense of relief. 'I always knew these mass graves existed,' Hall-Harper said. 'We are pleased with the fact there is some evidence mass graves have been located. We are excited about the next steps of uncovering a cover-up and laying these bodies to rest respectfully as they should have been nearly 100 years ago.'"

As that suggests, there is still plenty of work to be done before there has been a full accounting for the worst race riot in American history.

Online Resources

Other books about 20th century history by Charles River Editors

Other books about the Tulsa race riot on Amazon

Bibliography

Brophy, Alfred L. (2002). Reconstructing the Dreamland: The Tulsa Race Riot of 1921, Race Reparations, and Reconciliation. New York: Oxford University Press. ISBN 0-19-514685-9.

Scott Ellsworth, Death in a Promised Land: The Tulsa Race Riot of 1921, Baton Rouge, LA: Louisiana State University Press, 1992.

Rudia H. Halliburton, Tulsa Race War of 1921. San Jose, CA: R and E Publishing, 1975.

James S. Hirsch, Riot and Remembrance: The Tulsa Race War and Its Legacy, Boston, MA:

Houghton Mifflin, 2002.

Rob Hower, 1921 Tulsa Race Riot: The American Red Cross-Angels of Mercy. Tulsa, OK: Homestead Press, 1993.

Hannibal B. Johnson, Black Wall Street: From Riot to Renaissance in Tulsa's Historic Greenwood District. Austin, TX: Eakin Press 1998.

Tim Madigan, The Burning: Massacre, Destruction, and the Tulsa Race Riot of 1921. New York: Thomas Dunne Books, 2001.

Lee E. Williams, Anatomy of Four Race Riots: Racial Conflict in Knoxville, Elaine (Arkansas), Tulsa, and Chicago, 1919–1921. Hattiesburg, MS: University and College Press of Mississippi, 1972.

Free Books by Charles River Editors

We have brand new titles available for free most days of the week. To see which of our titles are currently free, click on this link.

Discounted Books by Charles River Editors

We have titles at a discount price of just 99 cents everyday. To see which of our titles are currently 99 cents, click on this link.

Made in the USA
Coppell, TX
22 June 2020

28801181R00024